BUT WHAT:
SELECTED POEMS

FIELD TRANSLATION SERIES 13

Judith Herzberg

BUT WHAT:
SELECTED POEMS

Translated by Shirley Kaufman
with Judith Herzberg

Introduction by Henk Romijn Meijer

Oberlin College Press:
FIELD Translation Series 13

Early versions of these translations have appeared in
*Field; Midstream; A Book of Women Poets from Antiquity to
Now*, ed. by Aliki Barnstone and Willis Barnstone,
Schocken Books, N.Y., 1980; *Dutch Interior*, ed. by
James S. Holmes and William Jay Smith, Columbia
University Press, N.Y., 1984; *Voices from the Ark*, ed. by
Howard Schwartz and Anthony Rudolf, Avon Books,
1980; *Quartet*, Wilfion Books, Paisley, Scotland, 1978;
Modern Poetry in Translation (England); and *Nine Dutch
Poets*, City Lights Books, San Francisco, 1982.

We are especially grateful to Scott Rollins who shared
some of his unpublished draft translations with us.

Peter Burger's careful reading of this entire manu-
script and his incisive and crisp corrections and com-
ments were extremely useful.

These poems were first published in Dutch by G.A.
van Oorschot, Amsterdam.

We wish to thank the Foundation for the Promotion of
the Translation of Dutch Literary Works for a grant to
help us complete this book.

Library of Congress Cataloging in Publication Data
  Herzberg, Judith (translated by Shirley Kaufman
  with Judith Herzberg)
    But What: Selected Poems
LC: 87-043198
ISBN: 0-932440-24-X
    0-932440-23-1

CONTENTS

from **Dagrest**

New Poems

INTRODUCTION

THE SHADOW UNDERNEATH

Strong emotions are the source of poetry. True, but it is equally true that they are a threat to it. Allowed free play, the emotions must live within the hallucination of themselves. Judith Herzberg's poetry keeps a tight rein on feeling, understating what could become shrill or even disturbed. It is not a poetry of gaudiness or heroic stances. Take an early poem like "Park" that records the discovery of a truth that frightens its discoverers, a couple a "we," or more likely, one of this "we." It begins: "Walked and talked of things we'd later . . ." Where better than in a park, in nature ordered by humans for protection and enjoyment? A park is like a sea that will not let you drown, ideally suited for the carefree speculation about the future, "our" future. Such innocence is volcanic, so the poem stops short of naming plans. Instead, a view of life obtrudes itself: "to live is to move and to move is/a slow extended shiver." Although we may shiver in parks, they are not laid out to impose such a vision. It must have been there, this vision, at the back of the thinking mind, stronger than the temptation to forget, strong enough for the park to be seen in its image: "Stormtrees above us strain their branches." The park is felt to be menacing, a reminder of what it was meant to make us forget. The idea is expressed in a concrete image: "Under this park hangs/white, windstill in the ground, an unlit/other-park, where scaly animals/meet rarely dragging their feet." In the rush to a possible "later" we refuse to examine the present from which this "later" must grow. And, by extension, the "other-park" may well be a vision of our civilized living together.

The early poems particularly often stress the need to see clearly and draw conclusions only from what has been truly observed and experienced. The insights thus acquired are considered to be a worthier guide than metaphysics. The poem "Nearer" begins: "To know there are rhododendrons on the slopes of the Himalayas/is not enough." Learning, in other words, must not be a substitute for what can be detected with one's own eyes in one's own back-yard, as it were:

> To see a green beetle crawl
> on a shiny leaf see it fall off
> in the shadow underneath to recognize
> the color of the earth

not once or twice
but year after year, not on the slopes of
   the Himalayas
but here with this grass, this earth
and thus to know a small part of a larger
land . . .

The poem stresses this need as a condition for gathering self-knowledge, and in the elaboration of this idea the poem becomes almost didactic:

Later to be able to say: this is me,
I come from that piece of the country —
instead of having only the trek
for a hinterland . . .

There is merit in ideas, but they must always be rooted in this "small part of a larger land" which is, in Wallace Stevens's words, "all of paradise that we shall know." Keeping your mind open for what is there if you care to look, listening carefully, this may lead to an experience of essences, as in "Commentaries on the Song of Songs": "And I recognize, after Chateillon (1544),/Grotius (1644), Lightfoot, Lowth,/to my amazement Solomon."

It is the prominence of the tangible world that characterizes Herzberg's poetry, and reveals her desire to capture the most fleeting, the briefest of moments, when the law of gravity seems suspended, as in "Upbeat," another poem in her first book:

> Before every swing
> (in music as well)
> a moment of
>   nothing.
>
> Gibbons fall upward
> from branch to branch
> before they grasp they
>   don't.

Then a moral emerges:

> Befriending's
> not a matter
> of persistence but of
>   pause.

The transition suggests a logical link which is in fact not there. It is an association, rather, triggered by painfully careful observations. The link is more capricious than logical. And in all her work following these early poems, the scrupulous attention to physical detail brings a toughness of form and language that is there, no matter how elusive the subject. Judith Herzberg's poetry has remained impervious to the example set by the freely associative Dutch experimental poets who still governed the scene when her first book appeared in 1963.

Although the war may well have played a decisive part in directing the poet's sensitivity to the "shadow underneath," in making her perceive the "markers for dynamite" (in the poem of that title) in seemingly undisturbed nature, the poet herself never makes this claim. Judith Herzberg was old enough to have a conscious knowledge of the terrible period that came to an end in 1945, old enough to know that her parents were not where she had a right to expect them (she was hidden by a Dutch family during the German occupation of Holland while her parents were taken to a concentration camp), but there is no hint in her poetry of an exploitation of this subject. The war is present in a few poignant poems, a memory of rejoining her mother who has become a stranger ("Reunion"), or of words exchanged with a German pastor ("Bad Zwischenahn, 1964") who, asked "why his church honors the heroes of the First War/not those of the Second with a plaque," answers: "It doesn't come easy for any of us/to fit into ourselves and go on." Or, in an even more concentrated form, in "May Fourth," which in Holland is the day of the commemoration of the dead, when just before eight o'clock at night a two minutes' silence is observed throughout the country. In this silence one may hear what is normally drowned by the more familiar, louder noises, and these weaker sounds are not soothing or peaceful:

> Wind scraped the corners
> awnings flapped hinges squeaked.
> And in the empty air flags
> cracked like whips.

More capricious than logical. It seems to me true for many of the sometimes witty, sometimes sad ideas and the way in which they are linked. It is true for a beautiful poem like "A Late Encounter I" which takes the idea of "Park" a step further: "how to manage the limp/under a fuller sun when the last heat is caught,/arm in incomprehensible arm along the esplanade?," and it is true for the equally beautiful "A Late Encounter II" that strikes a perfect balance between what must be said and what must be left unsaid. The language captures the mind's whims without making statements about them. The poem steers clear of the beaten path, it moves away a little from official grammar, it is a little twisted, off-beat, quirky in a way that is both meaningful and very hard on the translator. Subjects are suppressed, sentences left unfinished, a new word is formed now and then (such as *groeierigheid* in "The Day-After Pill" which is a little quainter than *growingness*), or a word is treated in an unusual way (such as *kwijt* that is given a comparison, translated here as "loster").

Searching for an English equivalent for such stylistic idiosyncrasies, I thought of the first sentences of Muriel Spark's novel *The Bachelors*: "Daylight was appearing over London, the great city of bachelors. Half-pint bottles of milk began to be stood on the doorsteps of houses containing single apartments from Hampstead Heath to Greenwich Park . . ." The bottles that "began to be stood" add something graphic, they are alive, spied on and caught in the act by an amused eye. I know why they are there and yet I would not easily find something equally effective in Dutch.

Anyone who has ever been close to the problem is aware of the "impossibility" of translating poetry, which is all the more reason to be grateful to Shirley Kaufman, who was willing to undertake such a hazardous task with the poet herself, and has admirably retained the strength of these poems. This book is an introduction to some of the finest poetry written in Dutch today.

Henk Romijn Meijer
Amsterdam.   November, 1987

from **ZEEPOST**
(1964)

MAGIC

Before the war it was different —
boxes full of pointed Caran d'Ache
in all the colors of the rainbow,
but if you slid them open
      everything changed because
before the war there might be a war.

Look how sweet children
look how sweet we were
we locked our mothers in the cellar
blew up frogs with a straw.

And when we slid those boxes open
fireworks jumped out on parachutes
that were shot down at once
and falling, scratched the sky.

So it was all
our fault
she told us so.

NEARER

To know there are rhododendrons on
    the slopes of the Himalayas
is not enough. To see a green beetle crawl
on a shiny leaf see it fall off
in the shadow underneath to recognize
    the color of the earth
not once or twice
but year after year, not on the slopes of
    the Himalayas
but here with this grass, this earth
and thus to know a small part of a larger
land, so huge it might be called motherland
mother Russia, mother Europe.
Winters, when clouds stand
at the window, homesickness in precise
    detail,
leaves, each vein complete in them.
Later to be able to say: this is me,
I come from that piece of country —
instead of having only the trek
for a hinterland, like a nomad, only gravel
along the railway, a breath of scorched
earth for the smells of childhood, as stake
for a new start only the fact
that scorched earth can still be planted.

COMMENTARIES ON THE SONG
OF SONGS

After Rabbi Akiba, Buxtorf, Herder,
mature men who are serious but dead,
who have paged through, consulted, held
        meetings,
but read what they wanted to see,
now it's me with my little eyes
bent over earlier texts
(reading more leather-bound books
as my own death comes closer).
And I recognize, after Chateillon (1544),
Grotius, (1644), Lightfoot, Lowth,
to my amazement Solomon.

Hello love from the middle
of a body and the middle of a life,
closely heard and closely spoken
breath felt and skins smelled —
we are sailing under the same flag.

ON THE DEATH OF SYLVIA PLATH

We stand naked behind the line
those in front try to hide
those in back press forward.

They're bidding over us
the frightened ones have most to fear
nobody knows what she is chosen for.

I've heard the bad news
having saved my own skin miraculously
I'm mourning now for my sister.

Mene tekel is a beast
an ant a crab and crawls with black
claws from the cinders onto the hot tracks.

Consolation for the roofless never
comes in the form of houses
but from the mouths of nomads.

For the astonished child
who was born anyway
space does not turn inside out.

It must find refuge with the wolves
if such motherly wolves
still exist.

THE VOICE

Translated into language it is something
     like this:
a voice, sweet as a saxophone
that comes leaping from a great distance
over mountains, over me
like the voice of Solomon —
makes me tremble like the tower
when the bells ring
"when we no longer ding-
dong, what will we do?" or like
the rib cage of a frightened dog.

A voice that says with jazz, with Solomon,
that we must either be on edge
or not at all, or not at all.

OURSELVES AND OUR PLANTS

Ourselves and our plants are the only
        things
coincidental in this house. The rest is all
intended as it is, if not by us, then
by someone who thought for instance
it should be rectangular, or cotton.
Nothing can be done about this.
If there weren't so many options
we could lick each other artlessly
the way we do a shell, the faceless
soles of our feet, and cat-like
rasp the breast hair. Sometimes
I surprise your face smiling at someone
through thick cobwebs of chair backs
and heads and hands holding glasses.

PARK

Walked and talked of things we'd later —
to live is to move and to move is
a slow extended shiver.
Stormtrees above us strain their branches.

Under this park hangs
white, windstill in the ground, an unlit
other-park, where scaly animals
meet rarely dragging their feet.

OLD AGE

Later, when I am feeble-minded,
with a lapdog and goose skin,
I'll keep a bottle warm
against me and talk
to you in my sleep.
If you can understand now
what I'm going to say then,
crackling withered stem that I'll be,
I will not feel so broken off,
more like a blown-out dandelion.
Can you hear me babble?
There go my little parachutes.

UPBEAT

Does the little boat
on the crest
of a wave stand
   still?

And the mast,
to and fro, after
to, before
   fro?

Before every swing
(in music as well)
a moment of
   nothing.

Gibbons fall upward
from branch to branch
before they grasp they
   don't.

Does a showhorse
when about to
jump, hold
   back?

Befriending's
not a matter
of persistence but of
    pause.

Silence decides
the tone. As in
Eskimo
    songs.

ISLAND

There's something sad about sadness
as if it weren't enough by itself.
Calling under water
for what's not there.
It seems to wear off, time
shoves it away.
REINDEER DYING FROM HOMESICKNESS.
Homesickness for the unlimited
tundra of the north.
It is not that on Öland
they can't run, they cannot
get used to the idea
that everything always ends in that sea.

from **BEEMDGRAS**
(1968)

BURYING

Would he understand that I wasn't at his grave
because I had a cold, if I had a cold?
And would he know this was an easy out
and nod at me, yes naturally, and of course
I didn't have to? That it was no use hearing
the rain on his box, that he himself
wouldn't be there except for his . . .
He with his little table-lamp pocket-scissors
        thermostat
who kept doors closed against the draft, eyes open
especially for the uncurling of soft leaves,
ears only for the cheerful twitter
of budgies in the aviary. Would he
understand, if he still understood,
what brought me here, under these improperly
        hurried
clouds, while he couldn't attend?

REUNION

For years I had not seen such a town
or stood at the bottom of such stairs
as on that hot day, in black Sunday best
and leather shoes. And at the top
I saw vaguely my strange mother
I'd have to give her a kiss.

Soft cuddling that night after night
I'd pretended, to creep from
the war into sleep,
was dividing us now. Too grown-up,
too skinny and countrified, I took
it all back. Was this
really my mother?

Come up, she said,
winking to put me at ease,
but with both eyes at once.
Right then I thought we should say
the goodbyes we'd delayed,
but I didn't know how to look at her
with my difficult eyes.

MAY FOURTH

Just when he was about to say:
but everyone provides himself with problems
not so large he can't see past them
to an unattainable, better life,
it was time for the two minute silence.
Engines were turned off
churchbells stopped ringing
and birds, swarms of starlings,
whizzed over the square.
Wind scraped the corners
awnings flapped hinges squeaked.
And in the empty air flags
cracked like whips.

WE LIVE

We live off the intentions of our intentions.
Not one cell or papilla is the same
in this our present year
as in that while ago, our start.

We equal forty-two generations of mice,
maybe more. Probably more.
They live fast and small. Not one
of fourteen years ago is still around.

And yet, even these great-
great grandchildren
of our primal feelings and designs —
they got the message.

They rustle behind dry wallpaper
and scramble over the floor.

VOCATION

And when they asked her what she wanted to be
she said, "Invalid, please," and saw herself
in brownish plaids, her legs not moving,
pushed by a loving husband and pale sons.
Not even a stamp to paste,
not a letter to write, no trip to take.
Then she'd really be free,
look as sad as she'd like, be first
in the shops, up front
at parades, not wear pretty clothes.
And every night she'd sob softly
and say, "It's not for myself
but for you."
Both boys would stay
with her always, devote
their lives to her, and nothing
would ever happen to her, she would
never, never wear out.

MARKERS FOR DYNAMITE

Almost fell back to talking again, the kind
that doesn't admit love to loving
but frays, so I got myself into the night
to look at the leaves. A gull,
out late for food, passed bleating softly.
There were leaves. And pale blue numbers
     suddenly
on the rocks, markers for dynamite.
It was so quiet that in that quiet
I rolled up inside, opposing this.
What good does it do to widen the trail?
To chop the birches that root in the past?
                        Would you rather
belong to the engineers pulling at progress?
Still there's this shifted, constant trust
in rocks and earth, so surely part of us
almost as if holy, as if stone had meaning
(the old man coming off the plane
kneels, kisses his holy land,
but only his mouth is holy). No,
these transfixations of the soul are less
us than the first inching of warmth.

Dearest, sadness aside, I'm running back,
isn't it amazing how after a sun's been down
so long, bellies of the highest gulls
still catch the light?

YIDDISH

My father sang the songs
his mother used to sing,
to me, who half understood.

I sing the words again
nostalgia flutters in my throat
nostalgia for what is mine.

Sing to my children
what I myself don't grasp
so they may later. . . . later?

We had to throw the roses out.
We needed the water to drink.

Sad intimate language
I'm sorry you withered
in this head.
It no longer needs you
but it misses you.

BAD ZWISCHENAHN, 1964

The bride hobbles out of church on too high
    heels
and smiles her chafed smile under topheavy hair
and lets herself be kissed by the uncles and stands
between the graves and looks her small new
    husband in the eyes.

Begonias burst into bloom, ivy grows
up the medieval churchfront,
all for the sake of the photographer.
Now the pastor can explain
the old altar-piece to us.
The man beating Jesus must keep roaming,
he is the Jewish people, the wandering Jew
last seen, according to legend, in Bremen, 1510.

I swallow and ask him in this warm and stifling
    Germany
why his church honors the heroes of the First
    War
not those of the Second with a plaque.
He speaks for himself, me, god,
    the photographer, the dead:
It doesn't come easy for any of us
to fit into ourselves and go on.

KINNERET

The water does not lie heavy and deep
but hangs as mist between the mountains
a safety net stretched to its limits
and hooked to the points of light
visible here and there along the coasts.
A net for stars?
Not one of them falls, the sky is solid enough
but there is so much to wish for
around this charged and waiting water
where peace was preached more often
than anywhere else
and conquerors,
strong as tornados, left their
marks in the form of ruins. Gods
differ. Even tonight
rifles take aim:
for each light another light
it wants to stifle.

April, 1965

PRESENCE

Nothing is old or has been old.
The pyramid is there, so is the pod
but old is old if you choose to think old
and that is in the now and for a moment.
His hand goes through his hair,
not absentminded,
no, the opposite.

INTERESTING NOVELTIES

He came in to fiddle with the knobs,
fumble with the tubes,
and talk me into some new
kind of ventilation stabilizer,
promising that if the whales
would ever actually die out something
very special and just as ingenious
would be invented, wait and see.
Like what? A more spontaneous leviathan?
Don't forget, he said, that we found margarine.

THE DECISION IS PENDING

Pending the decision
pending the house
pending the furniture
pending the children
the drop pends
young and with a purpose.

When the drop falls
the children will fall
the furniture will fall
the house will fall
and the decision.

In another five days
it will be five years.

IN A BOOK

after a painting by Dubuffet

In a book of reproductions,
an asphaltic painting:
two small creatures
start to wipe out memories.

Creatures, though gray
and barely outlined, still
owners of a past
in which they did the kind of things
"they'd be sorry for."

It's the only way:
get into a black and white
picture, lively but vague
wipe as though you are leaving,
wave goodbye and do not move.

from **STRIJKLICHT**
(1971)

SENTENCED

Maybe more years are left to me
than this half to her.
What do I say? How
can you talk to someone who's going to die?
If only I could live a little faster
and quickly come back here
so I could tell her how it works there.
But through the spindles of the chair
I see some things on the table
looking permanent, and feel
that I'm feeling her envy.
Spindles are like outlines
and like doorposts and windows
and like binoculars and frame
afterwards just as before
what's living and still to be lived
what we're not yet
or no longer part of.

SNEAKERS

Just got used to
houses torn down
uncles stooped over
and even more stooped every year,
twelve-year-old airedales
put away,
got used, I mean,
not so much to the wearing out
as to "They've had their day."
Not so much to one's own death then,
disguised as somebody else's,
as to the ends of certain supports
that give out before we do.
No one hangs on to a strawberry.
Although, but now we're off limits
because if you start to think about a strawberry,
really, the way you sometimes
happen to think about a spider
after he's fallen 3 ×
in the same pail, and you've rescued him 3 ×
(the first time because you didn't want a dead
spider in the water, second time
because you'd already done it and third time
because you've gotten to know him)
well, just got resigned to the wilting I was

      saying
when suddenly I got a pair of sneakers
exactly like the ones I had ten years ago. Same
looks, design, laces.
So absolutely the same a second life
seemed possible. See how they walk
but with my legs my ankles my feet.

THE DAY-AFTER PILL

An unwanted person? So what,
you're polite, you have been one
yourself, still are now and then.

Sometimes you see, through gray
curtains, a dead man driving
toward you, not him though.

Aren't we all in that difficult phase
of being older than before
and younger than we'll be?

Don't hesitate too long
the smaller it is the longer it takes
to start kicking around.

Now it is nothing but growingness
an old man who isn't here yet,
maybe a party-goods salesman?

Too small to imagine its form
and because of its tininess
too lost to make loster.

Less than frogspawn or eggshell,
not a sign of a prince,
just a me.

Such a small crayfish, thinner than
a gnat's wing, unfit to defend itself —
almost like everyone.

BEAR IN BED

Ah yes, I had a bear,
a bear had me, and for the first
time in my house someone
was having his way. In the dark
I came home from chopping wood,
pulled off my boots in the corner
where I sleep, but it stank
strange, of animal.

It was a fat, wet fur
but no, it grumbled.
There was no budging it.
An uncomfortable night.

In the morning
on his way out
he drank my week's supply
of sour milk,
licked the bottom clean
upsetting the bucket,
and then stepped carefully over it.

It was roomy when he had gone.

In the evening he came back,
shook himself dry
so the drops hissed in the fire.

Good evening, I said.
He stepped lightly again,
only the rap rap
of his nails on clay.

Tell me what you did
today, have you eaten
did you hunt?

For the first time someone
in that house had his way:
lay down, fell asleep.

I was up already
sitting on the doorstep
when he came outside
with his small discontented eyes.

The sun shone
and the bear disappeared
in the direction of Zilina.

At night he came home,
I gave him new milk
I'd fetched in the valley
and asked: what did you do?
Meet a she-bear?

He moved into my daily life
staying on and on,
and I'll never find out
what else he did.

I was sharpening my axe
in the yard to store
wood for the winter when a hawk
circled over our heads.

Traitor, spy, ally?

I didn't know but somehow
without looking up
the bear got a message.
He waited awhile.
Made a quick turn.

Loosely on his easy legs
he lumbered into the wood
and disappeared.

How did it get to this
from always coming to sleep
to never wanting to meet?

I searched in the woods,
but all god's dumb bucks
all dried-up brooks
blown-off branches
cloud stripes and rock cracks
pointed the wrong way.

Then the first snow came
and I gave up,
stumbled back in the cold
hoping without hope
I'd find him at home.

Where did he come from?
Is that where he'd gone?
How can I save him
from traps or whatever
if he's not where I've searched
two nights and two days?

Shot, dragged half dead
through the snow

maybe bought and already
sold?

SKIMMING LIGHT

on the torpor and swiftness of gulls

They have the thoughtful arctic glide
hahaha from up high a slow
drift or the quick
and meddling blabber of goats.

They hang in one place so long
their shadows are glued to the rocks.

At dusk when the ground is still warm
and only the sea is lit, they spatter
from the luminous cliff like sparks from a fire.

FIREPLACE

Warmth keeps us together. Instead
of the 6 o'clock news, there's this
to look at, flashing hot.
It grips and comforts.
Like a cockfight on the eastern front.

1944

Be glad you are still alive,
and was and was but sang
my body lies over the ocean.

And looked up at the birds
in their quivering summer.
Crossbills, orioles
were still around
and kingfishers over the ditch.

Radar averting tinsel
brilliantly woven through their nests.

A joyful summer, full
of green promise, they flew
wherever and back again
wherever they wanted in their peace,
gulls even over the sea.

1945

We were having heroes to tea
they sat together on the sofa.
They didn't have a thing
to say. I stared and stared
till they were very shy
they had no way of coping
with such peace.

QUARTZ MICA FELDSPAR

See farther than I can see a sea
longer than I stay. Vanish
self sitting on a rock of ever-
till-never longer than time.
Higher and lower than I can think songs
notes more insisting than my presence.
Say nothing for a while with a voice of
      elsewhere in this
extended hereness this
matching against air water gneiss
between getting born and lost
say nothing for a while, that's how long it will
      last.

MIDWINTER SOMEWHERE ELSE,
MORE SOUTH

It's quite a hardship for him
to step like that from his car
among corduroy fields, snow in the ruts,
trees that, in whitish light, underline themselves.
Whitish not white. April light in December.
He doesn't know winters with this light it's
      forced
not real, not really his. Feelings are hard
to pack up. Just like
his life in a longhouse on the border
with the customs officer who, between import
      and export,
keeps watch in the corridor, puts his finger
down to the bottom of each cup of soup
he takes from the kitchen to his room.

STARLING

Claimed nothing whatever
too small for feathers
too wet to be called brown
and beak too fastened
to get food down.

But became an extremely
warmlegged scholarly
highly specialized
seal feathered
shoelace fanatic,

frivolthroated imitator,
pearl spattered
weasel, a flying
analphabatic celebrator.

JACKDAW I

No more blue membrane that slid over his eyes
while he wearied on his stick.
Two worms crawl in his cage,
he's no longer alone now, has food,
food that lives, food that curls around his beak,
he is the boss now, boss of the cage,
boss of the grass that's moving.
Now he is ready to drink some water,
sharpen his beak, smooth his feathers, now
the dirt crackles again.

JACKDAW II

He hates to sleep in a cage.
When evening comes on and begins to blow
he wants the clouds but doesn't know
that he can't fly, only
that he wants to fly. Wants to fly. He keeps
a bead eye on the bars,
as soon as he sees his chance he'll go
but doesn't know that cats lie waiting
under shrubs. Hard beak
half open, he won't eat, hacks
holes in the stick where he sits.
He's alone, black, an alien
like the Greek, who, with his broken leg,
wants to get out into the air
where the girls are, turns on
the radio next to his cot:
insulting music from far away
like the caw! caw!
of jackdaws hanging on the wind.

SWIFT

Head level as an eagle's head
eyes deep and sharp and sad
he lies simply, so unsimple
for one who lives such an aerial life,
on our steps. He claws
my hand with predator nail needles.

Like a toy airplane
he taxis around our floor
as if a wheel were missing,
in crooked circles, around.

If angels exist this is one.
Unearthly and outlandish,
never belonging here,
he can't even start up like this,
he needs air to float on
as he falls, high ledges to grip.

His eyes have two slanted
screens that slide
and eyelids slow as a doe's.
His beak is broad and quick and pointed,
geared to gnats, and like a Stradivarius
finished with two f-slits.

A flat birdlouse crawls
out of his feathers now and then,
a tiny strangling hand.

He doesn't know a soul
or the dangers of the ground,
he is not skittish or shy,
when he doesn't want to be here
he closes his eyes.

Back into the air with him
you say, but he falls in a puddle,
a small anchor of feathers.

LATE

We are a cloud
raked by a hoe.

We are a needle
on the turntable without a record.

We are drowned sparrows
fished from the rain barrel.

We are little old men
who drop their packages in the street.

We are the newest comedy
but the safety curtain won't go up.

We are stale bread
going in a small cart to the zoo.

We are the iron filings
left by the barbed wire machine.

We are tomato flowers
in our buttonholes and will never grow up to be
tomatoes.

LINES WRITTEN DURING LOCAL PEACE

The ones who still wanted to get onto their feet
    could,
fear-armored, climb out from under, not
    undamaged.

War — we are hardly ever heroes without it.

Protect the sleepy raindays
the soil which never had admirers.

Heroes — there is hardly ever a war without
    them.

Not something they describe as a miracle
more like the swallows so swedish and safe.

Peace — we are hardly ever heroes without it.

"Dearest, please store my tools in the attic
you can always give them to someone."

Heroes — there is hardly ever peace without
    them.

from **BOTSHOL**
  (1980)

POLITICAL CONSCIOUSNESS

The most terrible images, he said, don't
let go of me any more. I can't sleep,
he said, his head in his hands.
And poor drunken Jan
with his arms full of boxes full of apples
had to find his own way out the door.

We who are here lie awake,
see a chair on top of a wall
a flag flapping on a tree
a boy with a boy's hands.

He who is there is fast asleep
dreaming he is here and everyone whole.
Right now he wants to get up, hold the door
      open
for someone with boxes of apples.

TOURIST

The ground refuses my attachment.
I didn't grow anything here, except
one little plant on a grave, a fuchsia,
not hardy. I'd have to start
believing in god if I wanted
to leave my bones here. Too late
for the view that should be
enjoyed now, but isn't.

The most dazzling graveyard I know,
in this armpit of rock next to the sea.
It smells of hay, hay
for which I have no cow.

TRAVELACHE

All right, you can come with me, come
and explore, clamber over old
toppled cities, and from the tall
present day, sunrise — sunset —
where shall we eat.

You can go in the suitcase,
between the folds of my skirts,
in the holes of my beads.

But will you, will you please,
please behave? Because
we're going to meet someone there,
someone who doesn't know you yet.
I'll introduce the two of you,
but composed, not wild
like before.

On a balcony, maybe,
considerate and calm,
towards evening, glasses
with ice cubes
that tinkle maybe.
And please don't think you hear
the big freeze cracking.

Go to sleep early and quietly, promise
to dream about small and close.
Don't wake screaming in the night.
No more excesses.

No radio first thing in the morning.
Just the local singing,
with words we don't understand.
Not the news that grips the throat,
not what you call "the world."

And when we stroll in the easy valley
leave the images alone.
Don't make it happen over again:
the muck, the shouts.
The hills over there
can't help it.

A LATE ENCOUNTER I

Will there be a neat, white fence between
        their two
such different wildernesses? A gate that opens
        with a squeak?

Will their lips ease the distance, lips formed
        from such different
food, shaped from such different language?
Mouth to mouth each separate story straining
        with words.

Will it flow together, into one, how?
        When water
pours down from such different storms?

Touching, recognizable, the other's battered
        remains?
And the swamp fire there, flaring wherever
        it's stamped out,
uncatchable, not to be doused — will it always
        make trouble?

Each self only used to its own self — how to
        manage the limp
under a fuller sun when the last heat is caught,
arm in incomprehensible arm along
        the esplanade?

A LATE ENCOUNTER II

She says: look how
in the tent of our bed
our legs stretch out
to where the light
comes through the sheet and how our feet
already know each other.

*

All right then, shoes, downstairs along the carpet
the lobby the palms the coffee
into the street. France
underfoot. Snow? Do you feel the crunch
crunch as in novels translated
from Russian?

*

We don't have to understand
the language of our feet.
But at the waterfall
where we were speechless
our feet stood still
lingered impressed
then, together,
went on.

She has this craving for —
doesn't he? No,
if there's anything — yes?
— it may be May.
May somewhere else
but doesn't mention it.
What makes you sigh, love?
(remembers taxi)

*

What about that taxi?
The man beside me said
"If only it were April" and died.
And when I was a child I saw
wild horses scatter on the horizon
like a rain of seeds. Do you understand.
Me? What can she compare it to.

*

The story of my life
is it — is that what it is
is it really a story.

Strange, strange.
While you look, how do you look?
How take in, how compare?

*

And your dream?
I was driving.
A long straight road.
An empty landscape on both sides.
I am married.
I live alone.
I am not happily married.
I am very married.
I own a sofa.

*

What can she add?
The way she scratched the linen
with her nail.
But that's even less
of a story, and, like cart tracks,
sandmarks, impossible
to translate.

*

What's left gets shorter.
If only we could have a past
one pillow for two heads.

His heart rears and pulls
as if it wants out on its own
wants to bounce
down the road ahead of him.

*

His hand beside hers
but veined differently, weathered
by that different climate over there.
She looks, stares until no hand —
a small island rather, strange
never before, a strange map.

*

The way the sun goes down
the way he sees it
like a copper tray
she as a redhot
circular saw
at the end of the water hissing
as it spins down.

SONGS from
The Fall of Icarus

1 The Farmer

The worst is when everything stays as it is.
I can't and won't interfere I want
to go home milk the cows eat
and forget what I saw. The worst is
that this commotion, as if in a picture,
that this fall, of what?
of almost night by now
fixes me here.
My plow won't budge.
The worst is when even perishing
is painted down.

2 The Sailor

My wife, arms high, legs wide,
skirt over skirt should stand
at the end of the pier and cry with joy!

Joy's worn away from waiting so long.
Dried-up she sits on her straw mattress, dried-up
she looks at me.

It's days sometimes before she gets up.
I give her food, something to drink, sweet figs,
restrain my own voraciousness.

Then comes the marvelous melting,
then she starts moving again, spring!
— running, filling the buckets.

O holy Mary, right now when she's soft, right
     now
as we rest arms and legs around
each other, I sail again.

3 The Fisherman

There's addiction in my staring.
As soon as I cast, all the tossing
and searching inside me calm down,
my eyes rest on the bobber, but it's more
than that, as if I'm finally
allowed to stay in one place, and my gaze
gets stuck. I don't wait for a fish to bite.
I lock the moment. No obligations. Not even
to look. I limit myself to the ripples,
don't bother to go deep.
Apart from what appears or disappears
above or below, apart from what was
and what still has to be.
Slick colors shimmer in the nearest water,
much too much happening.
And look, here comes the first ripple
from some distant splash.
What's better than not doing anything,
not moving? Even the slightest
blink of an eye unsettles irrevocably,
and leads and leads to

UNTIL THEN WHEN IT ALL WENT WELL

Wealth is emptiness on shiny tiles
poverty is boxes with half-filled jars
rich a veranda with a view of nothing
poor a porch with planks and wheels
rich is not having to keep anything
poor makes do from winter to winter
richness is silence, silent behind silence
poverty rushes.

And so day and night they enjoyed
the silence, smooth water, white,
stony stones and the moss that was there.

DESERT

The wind, full of sand, scours the house
as if to round off the edges.

You dreamed you were dying, leg by leg,
I that you'd go away.
You went away.

I chose small tokens,
I gave you an eraser,
white, worthless, a Sahara present.

Time solves everything?
Sand buries it.

from **DAGREST**
(1984)

OVER THERE

Full of ideas about what it would be like,
they went there.

Seven layers of civilization, one
after another left in ashes.

It was so hot you couldn't
stand on stones for long.
"That's how bears learned to dance."

No spring, fall, twilight.
In the earth-dark they talked
about light, late light on rowanberry trees.

Less and less they lay together
felt their heartbeats:
but what but what but what.

GULLS

The shrieking of gulls pointed the way
    to the sea,
a steep alley down to the harbor,
nothing but boats, slow pulleys, cranes. No bird
flew or scavenged or rocked on a wave.
But the sound persisted, even the fury
    of machines
was dulled by the shrieking.
The cranes lifted crates, slightly open and light.
Between the chinks suddenly — a live cargo
    of wings
and feathers. That's how the gulls were hoisted
    into the hold.

CATS DON'T LIKE SUITCASES

A suitcase opens
on the smell of something
about to happen.

They'd rather not
go close to it,
but fear of bulk
makes them rub against it.

They avoid farewells
by taking off.

Pain they know,
not the passing,
that contradiction.

DAUGHTERS

From the smile you can tell that it's false.
But only after. The same smile four times
is too much, one less and it might
have been real. But whose smile should we
take away? Don't take anything away,
pull out the real from under the rubble
of obligations, beware of peril
in those rows of white teeth. If only
there were a woman with an ordinary
worried face. Smooth young worried.
But women can't afford such looks
especially not around him, the coward
who got himself out of the way bam bam.

HOW FAR

He always used to look out through the OO's
of his DOOR, but now there are glasses in front
of his eyes that enlarge the business.
Sometimes he knows he's a professor
and not a stupid one. There's so much to see
and *larger* may not be the right word.
More precise. Deeper. The most in the finest
detail. He sees the numbers on the farthest bus.
Or is it the farthest? Who says how far
a man is supposed to see, where is the limit?
This irks him. His eye-hunger is aroused
and even if he sees more sharply the wrinkles
in his skin, the seeing itself is younger.
He would like to take the whole optician's guild
in his arms and embrace it, same as he always
wanted to squeeze his mother especially
when he felt that because of her he belonged
to the whole world and the other way round
    a little.
He considers binoculars and a microscope.
There's still so much more, but he sees the
    meaning
of his life when he comes home, stares up
from his bed and makes out the newest crack
in the ceiling. That's how far it is.

AFTER THE BATTLE

Always
the empty cartridge of a house,
windows nailed shut with slats
or cardboard, one, upstairs,
completely open. There
the yellow striped curtain
blows in, out.
Next to the wall,
a little away from it,
always the one undamaged
skinny chair.

PROGRAM

Fear wakes first. Then it wakes
Reason and the Program for the Day
that will tuck it in again. Why
can't Calmness get up first, or
Joy, why is Fear so unruly,
so pushy?
                    Teacher! Me! Me!
Yes, yes, the teacher has noticed. Now
go back to your seat and don't talk out of turn.
After lunch when we have history, you can
tell us all you want, what actually
has happened.

SHOES

Every morning, between putting on
his right and his left shoe,
his whole life quickly passes by.
Sometimes he almost doesn't
get around to the left one.

PAIN KILLERS

Could there be such a thing, a law
for the conservation of pain,
so that if we fight it now,
some other time there'll be a hurt
worse than the sound of *ow*?

Or does pain, like energy
(sorry, Analogy), transform itself
not into heat, but somehow
into a kind of freeze
worse than the sound of *ow*?

Or could it be the pain we drive out
takes on a different form,
unlaughed, unsung, disavowed,
stiffens our pain-thirsty bodies
aching for the sound of *ow*?

SONG

Don't lie to me please
about anything big, about anything
else. I'd rather know what was destroyed
than have you lie
because that's more destructive.

Don't lie about love,
something you feel or something you'd
like to feel. I'd rather
be sad than have you lie
because that's sadder.

Don't lie about danger
because I know your fears
and if I don't trust what I know
you'll be a stranger
and that's more dangerous.

Don't lie to me about sickness,
I'd rather look into that pit
than lose myself in one
of your sweet placations
because I'd lose myself even more.

Don't lie to me about dying
because as long as we're here
I find that blocked
unsharing of thoughts
worse and much more dead.

NEW POEMS

BLUE ANEMONES

Bunch of thirty blue anemones.
One has a few kinks in its stem,
at every kink a new angle.
The only flower that looks straight out.
Don't think this is the poet.
He doesn't know yet
which of the thirty is him.
Doesn't even know he's going to get
blue anemones.

DISTURBING THE PEACE

The raging next door has no end: so hounded
cornered in her own house in her
angular husband in her child in the child in her.

When I ask: why don't you leave?
she'd say if she were honest, but she isn't
she says, so I don't ask.

Then I'd say: It's the scariest,
a corroding acid eating everything
wherever you are you fall off.

Then she could say oh meaning
that's what you'd like, and I could say no
and think yes and not be able to explain.

THE WAY

The way you sometimes get to a room, not
        knowing why,
and then have to figure out what you were after,
the way you take something out of a closet
without feeling around for it and only after you
        hold it
know what you were looking for,
the way you bring a package somewhere
and when you leave are startled, feeling too
        light,
the way you wait for someone, fall madly
        in love
for a second with anyone passing, and still go on
        waiting.
The way you know I've been here once,
        what was it about,
until a smell comes back to tell you what,
the way you know whom to be careful with
and whom not, whom you can lie down with —
that's the way animals think, I think,
the way animals know the way.

BOXES

Because all through the war we always heard
about before the war and how naive
they were, I am very careful now.
If I throw out something, for instance
a carton, I hope
that box will never catch up
with me in the shape of blame:
just think how innocent,
to throw out boxes,
if only we'd kept one,
kept only one!

BECAUSE ENGLISH HAS NO *AU*

I'd rather declare
hocus pocus
than learn, sort of,
a language.
I know nothing except
what's exact about anything.
When I belch
it's in Dutch.
Or when I wordless
hand this over.

Summer asks
and winter answers,
also the opposite.
One doesn't heap roses
on roses.

Now the longest day is already gone again
and there hasn't been a cool
pale green breezy one
with unmown grass for you
to lie on a dike
looking at each other in yet.

NOTES

The Dutch titles of books in this volume are difficult to translate in one word, and were left in the original Dutch in the table of contents.

Zeepost Sea-mail, meaning by slow boat.

Beemdgras Fieldgrass, one of the most ordinary grasses which grows between pavement stones, etc. *Poa Pratensis* in Latin.

Strijklicht Skimming light, a slanted, low light, also called "edgelight" in film jargon. It is especially used to reveal textures.

Botshol A small lake near Amsterdam. It also means something like dodgemhole, or clashburrow.

Dagrest Rest of the day. A Freudian term meaning the snatches of daily reality that appear in dreams.

p. 35 "May Fourth" Date commemorating the dead of W.W. II.

p. 85 "Songs from *The Fall of Icarus*" are part of a libretto written for the Theater School in Amsterdam. Produced in 1980.

THE POET

Born in Amsterdam in 1934, Judith Herzberg makes her home in Amsterdam and Tel Aviv. She has published seven volumes of poetry: *Zeepost* (1963); *Beemdgras* (1968); *Vliegen* (1970); *Strijklicht* (1971); *27 Liedesliedjes* (1971), an adaptation of the *Song of Songs; Botshol* (1981); and *Dagrest* (1984).

Translations of her poetry in English have appeared in *Modern Poetry in Translation, Poetry*, collections such as *A Book of Women Poets from Antiquity to Now* (ed. by Aliki and Willis Barnstone, Schocken Books, 1980), *Voices Within the Ark* (ed. by Howard Schwartz and Anthony Rudolf, Avon Books, 1980), and several anthologies of poetry of the Netherlands, most recently *Dutch Interior: Post–War Poetry of the Netherlands and Flanders* (ed. by James S. Holmes and William Jay Smith, Columbia University Press, 1984). The editors of this anthology have called her "the foremost woman poet in Dutch."

Judith Herzberg has also written several plays for theater and television in Holland and Germany, and a number of film scripts. Her most recent film, *Charlotte*, based on the life of Charlotte Salomon, a young German-Jewish painter who died in Auschwitz, was produced in Germany and has been widely shown throughout Europe and the United States.

THE TRANSLATOR

Shirley Kaufman is an American poet from Seattle and San Francisco who has made her home in Jerusalem since 1973. She has published five volumes of her own poetry, most recently *From One Life to Another* (1979), and *Claims* (1984). She is also the author of several volumes of translations of Hebrew poetry by Amir Gilboa and Abba Kovner (Kovner's *My Little Sister and Selected Poems* appeared as Number 11 in the *Field* Translation Series, 1986).